INTRODUCTION TO [...] BREEDS

C000173878

If this book was about a pure breed of dog— Cocker Spaniels, Poodles, or Malamutes, for example— we would begin with a discussion of the breed's history. We'd examine how the breed came to be, the country of its origin, and the reasons for its development.

In the case of mixed breed dogs, however, we cannot do that. Mixed breed dogs are exactly as the name implies: they are not pure anything. Instead, their makeup is a collection of genes from two or more pure breeds or other mixed breeds whose genetic background no one can identify.

Some mixed breeds clearly show the identity of their parents. For example, we can see a dog born of a purebred Labrador Retriever and fathered by a different pure or mixed breed that looks strikingly like a Labrador. Yet that dog exhibits atypical Labrador behavioral traits. In this case, the dog looks like a Lab but acts like its father or ancestors on its father's side.

On the other hand, we see many mixed breeds that simply look like themselves and no other breed. The dog may be a product of two mixed breeds, one purebred and one mixed breed, or two different purebreds.

This mixed breed is showing his true colors—he is really an "All-American" dog!

In short, obtaining a mixed breed dog is a lot like buying a bag of jelly beans. You're going to get a variety of colors and flavors, some of which you may not like, but most of which will bring you pleasure.

Mixed breed dogs are often referred to as mongrels, mutts, or even curs, although that name implies unfriendly and often homeless mixed breed dogs. Possibly the most popular handle for mixed breeds in general is "All-American dog."

Like the all-American version of homosapiens, All-American dogs are created by mixing the backgrounds of the same species. And like their human companions, there are occasional misfits in the lot, yet most are surprisingly wonderful individuals who make living with them a joyous event.

Accepting the fact that we'll never really know the complete genetic makeup of a mixed breed, let's move on to some factors that we do know and how those elements can serve to help us understand a particular All-American dog. So for a glimpse into the possible size, appearance, and behavior of a mixed breed, we should take a comprehensive look at purebred dogs.

There are seven groups of purebred dogs that comprise most of the dog-world population and from which most mixed breeds descend. These are the groups and a brief description of original purposes for which they were bred.

Sporting dogs were bred to hunt with man. They retrieve fallen birds from the water as well as dry land. They flush out coveys of small birds, such as quail, so the hunter can shoot them as they take flight. These dogs are happy, enthusiastic hunters who respond easily to quick movements on the ground as well as in the air. Retrievers, pointers, setters, and spaniels are all part of the Sporting group.

Non-Sporting dogs are made up of dogs that no longer perform the jobs for which they were originally bred. The breeds in this group are as varied as their originally intended purposes. American Eskimo Dogs, Bichon Frises, Chows, Bulldogs, Boston Terriers, and Dalmatians are some of the breeds in this group.

Hounds are dogs that chase prey either by scent or by sight. Scenthounds use their noses to find small prey such as rabbits,

What a mixed bag of friends! In order to determine what the size and characteristics of your mixed breed will be, you need to know a little about the purebreeds in his genetic background.

Coochie, a combination of Cocker Spaniel and Poodle often called a "Cockapoo," is owned by Amy Rachman.

People who live alone, the handicapped, or people that live in places where medium or large dogs would find the living conditions impossible thrive on the companionship a Toy breed provides. Toy Poodles, Pomeranians, Chihuahuas, Maltese, and Yorkshire Terriers are all Toy dogs.

Herding dogs are bred to herd flocks of domestic animals such as cattle and sheep. They are hardy individuals, eager to work with man, and very intelligent. Shetland Sheepdogs, German Shepherd Dogs, Border Collies, Australian Shepherds, and Welsh Corgis are livestock dogs that have been serving man for centuries.

Working dogs are bred to be man's helpers in his work. They pull sleds, guide blind people, and

ground-dwelling rodents, and foxes. Sighthounds chase down large prey by sighting them first and then running them down. Beagles, Bloodhounds, Afghans, Greyhounds, Whippets, and Irish Wolfhounds are among the breeds found in the Hound group. They are usually calm, gentle individuals that express a certain air of independence and self-containment.

Terriers go to ground to flush out and catch small rodents on farms and in fields. They are fearless, often small in stature, intelligent, and strong-willed dogs. Airedales are the largest terriers. Miniature Schnauzers, Fox Terriers, West Highland White Terriers, and Cairns are among the most popular in this group.

Toy dogs are tiny dogs bred to keep people company. Insignificant as this description may seem, they fill a very important need for many people.

An All-American can make a wonderful pet. This Pointer-Chow mix, named Jake, is owned by Alicia Persichilli.

guard and protect people and property. They perform police and law enforcement duties such as locating drugs and weapons. They range in size from medium to very large, yet all are strong and intelligent. Great Danes, Mastiffs, Siberian Huskies, Rottweilers, Doberman Pinschers, Boxers, and Akitas are Working dogs.

By understanding that mixed breeds, somewhere along the line of evolving, originated from some of these breeds, we are better prepared to "guesstimate" what to expect from an individual mixed breed. Remember that every mixed breed carries within him the genes of his forebearers.

Use this information as a guide to what you can expect in looks and behavior from a mixed breed. Keep in mind that many other elements contribute to the end result in the creation of a mixed breed companion, but a hint at the genetic makeup of an individual is a tiny window into his background.

Other factors such as environment, early socialization, and training are equally as influential as genealogy in creating the mixed breed companion.

Now let's explore how knowledge of a mixed breed's background can help us find and understand the dog of our choice. Let's say, for example, you're looking for a companion to accompany you on weekend hiking trips. Ideally you'd need a hardy dog of medium build, one that's intelligent and eager to stay close to you, yet one that also enjoys being outdoors

regardless of weather conditions. (In this case, a couch potato would never make it!)

A dog with working or herding instincts would be ideal. Though a sporting dog may be prone to running ahead of you for a quarter mile or more, his love of the outdoors and his tremendous stamina might outweigh his wandering habits, particularly if you keep him on a lead.

Now let's try another example. This time we'll consider a person who lives in a city apartment and has only a limited amount of time for long walks and lengthy sessions of fetching tennis balls in the park. This person should consider looking for a mixed breed who carries the genes of a Toy dog or a small terrier. All of these breeds are usually content with limited outdoor exercise, happy to hang out with their owners in the house (particularly on the sofa or bed!) and quite satisfied to play indoors with bouncing chew toys.

These examples are offered to suggest that considering the known (if any) genealogy of a mixed breed can go a long way toward finding the perfect dog for you. In the case of a totally unknown background, it becomes obvious that you must choose the dog based on what you see when you meet the dog and what your gut feeling about him tells you. However, be assured that some of these unidentifiable mutts make wonderful companions providing they have good temperaments and are in good general health.

Speaking of good health, let's take a moment and discuss what

These kids don't mind being in "mixed" company! Giving a home to a mixed breed puppy will provide you with hours of fun and companionship.

is referred to in the dog world as "hybrid vigor." Hybrid vigor can be easily understood by saying it's the circumstance of survival of the fittest as determined by nature.

Nature's natural selection process weeds out the unnecessary and the harmful but keeps the good and the useful. Thus when a litter of mixed breed puppies is born, nature selects only the hardy and the mentally stable to survive. (If weak and sickly individuals were to survive and procreate, the species would soon become extinct.)

In every animal shelter in the world there are mixed breed dogs that were born in garbage dumps, in back alleys, and in the woods. Yet despite the harsh beginnings,

some of these individuals survive and become good candidates for sharing a home with humans, provided they are socialized and trained early in life.

In the case of purebred dogs, reputable breeders produce puppies based on their knowledge of the breed and the individuals they are working with, and do so with caring concern for the puppies that mating will produce. They breed only those dogs that have desirable traits that should be passed on to preserve and perpetuate the breed and its original purpose.

Greedy, disreputable breeders, on the other hand, produce puppies strictly for profit. They give little regard to seeing that only the best of their breed survives. Instead they often interfere with nature's natural selection and minister excessive amounts of medical attention to weak or sickly puppies, thereby thwarting nature's plan. The resulting puppies frequently grow up to be sickly or ill-tempered dogs that should never be allowed to pass on their less than ideal genes.

Mixed breeds that survive this early weaning out process, however, are frequently found to enjoy good health throughout their lives with little or no hereditary problems such as hip dysplasia, juvenile cataracts, or hearing loss. (A dog in the wild would have little chance of survival with those serious health problems.) Thus the expression "hybrid vigor."

TYPES OF MIXED BREEDS

Categorizing types of mixed breeds is a tough play to call because every mixed breed is a unique individual unlike any other. Even puppies born in the same litter can vary widely in looks, temperament, and personality.

Within the pages of this book, you'll find photographs of many dogs that typify the vast range of

It has been proven that spending time with a dog can reduce stress and improve the quality of life. Spot, a Pekingese-Shih Tzu mix, and his owner Katherine Wilson would have to agree.

mixed breeds we see today. There are big dogs with short coats, little dogs that have a wiry terrier look about them, soft, fluffy dogs with long flowing hair that demands almost daily attention, and medium-sized dogs that fit somewhere in between all the others.

As diverse as their looks, there are equally differing personalities among All-Americans. Intelligence and willingness to socialize with humans are also dog specific, rather than breed specific, among mixed breeds.

Thanks to television and movies, we find many examples of mixed breeds doing all sorts of things to entertain the viewer. Big Benji-type dogs, and little fire balls like Spot are constantly out–thinking the human stars on the screen. Surely there are as many mixed breed stars as there are purebred ones.

You can be sure that everyone of those dogs have two things in common. They are intelligent and willing to work with people. Without those traits, they wouldn't be used because, no matter how handsome an individual, producers and financial backers aren't about to waste money and time on dogs that are difficult to get along with.

How you choose the type of mixed breed you want to live with is easy, providing you do your homework before you bring that new dog home. A little bit of careful thought and planning can mean the difference between success and joy or failure and misery for both you and the dog.

Can you imagine deciding on a puppy rather than an adult dog, choosing a tiny ball of fluff with big brown eyes that say "take me home," and finally ending up with a dog that weighs 95 pounds and is stronger than you are? Sadly, it happens all the time. And though you're heartbroken when you are forced to give up the dog you've come to love because he's just too much dog for you, it's even more of a disaster for the dog.

A dog such as this will probably end up in a an animal shelter where he may or may not be adopted into a new home. If the second owners do not or cannot train him, the dog will once again be shelter bound. But the next time, he may not get another chance and will, instead, be euthanized.

That's why doing your homework *before* you make your final decision is so important. The fact that you're reading this book shows that you're well on your way to accomplishing that.

At about eight weeks of age, Mr. Worf, a Chow mix, was found wandering in front of an artist's studio. He is now the loyal friend of David Hammel.

SELECTING THE RIGHT DOG FOR YOU

In this chapter we'll go over what I call "The Seven Steps to Sanity" when choosing a new dog. Incidentally, these steps are applicable whether you're considering a purebred or a mixed breed dog. After all, all dogs belong to the canine family.

First, you need to address each aspect presented in the seven

SEVEN STEPS TO SANITY

1. **What kind of a dog are you looking for?** A big one, little one? One with short hair or long? Remember that the more hair a dog has, the more grooming you'll need to do. Some breeds such as Poodle and Bichon mixes will require professional grooming several

All puppies are irresistible, no matter what their background. However, dog ownership is a big responsibility that should be considered carefully.

steps. Next, you must answer to your own satisfaction each question posed by that aspect. Only then will you be ready to go out and find yourself a new friend.

Be assured that, if you follow the seven steps, the probability of success with a dog that's "the best dog I ever had" will be very high indeed.

times a year.

Failure to groom a dog requiring this kind of maintenance will cause discomfort to the dog and a nuisance for you when its fur collects all manners of debris and knots. In addition, a dog that requires grooming will always look smarter when it's groomed regularly.

The time you want to spend grooming your dog should be considered before choosing an All-American. Rags is a Miniature Schnauzer mix who is kept groomed in a terrier-style haircut by owner Tara Glaze.

Short-coated dogs need grooming, too. However, a soft brush run over the coat several times a week will keep the hair clean and shiny and help the animal feel good. Neglecting a dog's coat, whether long or short, often creates skin problems that become almost impossible to cure and expensive to treat, to say nothing of the animal's suffering.

The ultimate size of the dog you're going to live with should depend on the kind of home you have as well as the lifestyle you live. A big, rambunctious dog is not a good candidate for a tiny apartment. Nor is a toy dog the best choice for someone who lives on a farm and wants the dog to spend his days outdoors. Instead, choose a dog that will fit comfortably into your particular situation.

Would you like a dog that's dominant or submissive? A dominant individual wants to run things, including you. This dog needs to learn early on that you are the pack leader, and that accepting you as leader ultimately makes him happy as opposed to constantly fighting you for the top dog position.

A submissive dog is the type that says, "I understand you're the boss and I'm willing to go along with the program." Whether you're choosing a young puppy or an adult mixed breed, there are ways to help you learn more about the type of individual you're considering.

When selecting a puppy from a litter, observe the puppies interacting with each other. The bully of the pack is the one who will likely grow up to be a very dominant dog. In the litter, he pushes and shoves his siblings, tries to gobble up the food first, often takes possession of toys, and excludes the rest of the litter from a chance to play.

The way puppies interact with each other can tell you a lot about their personalities. It's not hard to tell who is top dog here!

The submissive puppy is usually Mr. Easy Going. He accedes to the bully, yet is not afraid to let his littermates know when they've over-stepped the boundary of his tolerance. He is often more interested in people than other dogs and willingly seeks out attention from kindly visitors.

It's very important to understand the difference between the submissive puppy and the shy one. The shy puppy usually seeks distant corners for safety, choosing to avoid strangers and his more assertive littermates. When you pick up the shy puppy, he will often shiver and appear to be very uncomfortable in your arms. During meals and playtime, he will often stand back and observe the activity rather than assert himself by getting involved.

As a pet owner, it is essential to keep your dog's teeth clean by removing surface tartar and plaque.

You can test the puppies yourself to find the dominant and the submissive ones in a litter. Pick up a puppy and gently but firmly lay the puppy on its side. The dominant individual will struggle and squirm in resistance while the submissive one will lay quietly without a struggle.

Next, while the puppy is moving around, perhaps investigating something in the room call to him with a happy tone of voice as you clap your hands. "Here pup, pup, pup," makes an inviting sound and one that stirs his curiosity.

If he rushes over to you, praise him generously because he's just shown that he wants to be with you. The little fellow who ignores your call and "does his own thing" demonstrates a strong sense of independence and will require a lot more work from you to build a bond with him.

This mixed breed submits to his owner and receives an enjoyable tummy rub.

Note that it's most unwise to attempt this dominance/submissive laying down test on an adult dog. The dominant dog may object vehemently to a stranger forcing him to lay down and he may bite you!

Instead, crouch down and extend the back of your hand for him to smell. Carefully observe

The submissive adult will most likely attempt to make friends and show an interest in being with you. The dominant one may be friendly enough but will demonstrate his dominant nature by jumping all over you, even nipping at you and acting obnoxiously pushy. The shy dog will never make it to your side.

Make sure that the dog you choose will fit into your lifestyle and family situation.

how the dog handles meeting you. Talk softly and allow the dog time to approach you on his terms. Never move quickly or threateningly toward a dog that doesn't know you. Sudden unexpected movements can incite the dog's instinct to run away or defend himself, both of which are undesirable responses to your approach.

This is the dog to be avoided at all costs for it may never develop enough self-confidence to live in your busy world. Instead it will become a burden rather than a joy.

Ideally you'll be looking for a dog that's somewhere in between the above three types. One whose behavior says, "Hey, I like you." A friendly dog, curious, with self control, eager to watch and be with you, and one that demonstrates an eagerness to play and interact affectionately will make a wonderful companion.

Finally, you need to decide whether you want an active dog or a passive one. Either one of these types placed in the wrong environment will be miserable and make its owners unhappy, too.

Think of an active dog as being similar to an athletic child full of enthusiasm and energy. This dog will need lots of activity to keep him emotionally stable and happy. The passive dog equates to the quiet, self-contained child who is content to play quietly, read, or just sit back and watch the world go by.

Terriers, sporting and working breed mixes usually carry a high proportion of active genes. Toys, non-sporting and hound breeds frequently contribute more passive gene traits to an individual. In the case of herding genes, these dogs are tireless workers who need to keep busy and may even herd you and your family around the house on occasion.

Both active and passive dogs are a pleasure to know and can be fun to live with. Which type you choose should depend on your own personality and lifestyle. Just remember that your dog will hopefully live a long life and choosing a dog that compliments and matches his human companions will be the most rewarding.

2. **Let's think about your family for a few minutes.**

Obviously all members of your family should agree on getting a dog before you begin your search. It goes without saying that one dissenting member can make things pretty miserable for everyone else.

If there's someone in the family who isn't quite convinced that your home needs a dog, you might try some public relations work. Invite a friend who has a well-mannered dog to visit you. Then let that member observe how pleasant a nice dog can be to have around. Talk about other dog owners you know who enjoy the experience.

Point out the advantages of dog ownership. They keep you company, warn you of impending danger, guard your property, and provide a lifetime of pleasure just being themselves. Be sure to emphasize that every dog has his own unique personality and it will be exciting to observe how your new friend develops his.

3. **Next, consider your living facilities.** Do you live in a house with a yard? A city apartment? A condominium? A home in the country or the suburbs?

Be aware that sneaking a dog into an apartment that prohibits dogs will only end in disaster. Apartment building owners are not about to change their rules for you.

For example, I live in a condo with a small Poodle. The rules of my condo association say that a condo owner can have one pet under 25 pounds. I have seen people move in with big dogs and ultimately had to give up their

If you already have pets in the home, introduce your new puppy slowly and always supervise them closely. Like these two, they will soon become best friends!

pets or move because they did not abide by the rules that, incidentally, are lawfully enforceable.

What facilities will you have for exercising your dog? Do you have a fenced-in yard? Are you prepared to keep the area clean and free of excrement on a regular basis?

If you will have to walk your dog for exercise purposes, are you prepared to get up early everyday to take the dog out? Will you be able to come home every evening for feeding and exercise time?

If you are, are you willing to carry a baggie along and pick up stool for disposal when you return home? If your community has a law requiring pick-up, you can be heavily fined if you choose to disregard that law.

Do you have other pets in your home? A bird, perhaps? Or a cat? Another dog? How are you going to introduce the new member to the ones who already live with you?

Patience and small steps of acceptance are a must when developing harmony between critters in the home environment. Also, it's important to recognize that a new dog may find it extremely entertaining to chase your cat while the cat sees the new dog as a grossly undesirable intruder.

A pet bird such as a parakeet or large parrot who flies freely around the house may be in jeopardy from the playful antics of a dog. You must monitor the activities of your new dog and manage the behavior of all pets within your home. Failing to do so can end in tragedy for the pets and heartache for you.

One thing you must accept before you get a dog is that turning a dog loose to wander the neighborhood is absolutely unacceptable in our modern world. With an ever-increasing human population, millions of speeding cars on the road, and people who do not think kindly of free-wandering dogs, you are

Spaying or neutering your All-American will not only help control the pet population, it will lessen the risk of your dog contracting certain diseases.

inviting trouble unless you plan on controlling your dog from the very first day he comes into your life.

4. **Now let's get down to the nitty gritty and talk sex.** Will you pick a boy or a girl mixed breed? These options are interesting to consider and should not be taken lightly.

Controlling the exploding population of unwanted dogs is on everyone's mind today. It is a major problem faced by communities and animal shelters in every country. The fact that you're considering a mixed breed dog now or are already living with one demonstrates your concern. Sadly, though, there are millions of people who don't care and allow their pets to breed indiscriminately.

However, there is a simple solution to this problem—spaying and neutering. Spaying females and neutering males renders them unable to reproduce. The cost is reasonable and many humane societies offer monetary incentives to those who adopt dogs from their shelters.

Beyond the consideration of unwanted breeding, there are several other advantages as well. Spaying females prevents the twice yearly habit of coming into season and attracting males to your front door. Breeding puppies is an expensive and time-consuming job, one best left to professional breeders who have spent years studying bloodlines and standards of perfection for their chosen breeds.

In addition, spayed females are

usually gentle dogs, content to be home with you and who are not at risk for mammary cancer later in life.

For many years I was a breeder. Now, having retired from the kennel business, I spay all my female dogs and enjoy knowing that I don't have to worry about managing females in season anymore.

Neutered males are the best kind of males to have as pets. They lose the wanderlust habit of roaming the neighborhood looking for females. They are less aggressive, yet they retain their desire and ability to act as guardians and watchdogs for home and family. And as if that weren't enough reason to neuter, you won't have to worry about testicular cancer in their senior years.

Dogs require a great amount of care, attention and time. Be sure you are ready to take on the responsibility before bringing a new dog into your home.

You can spay females and neuter males anytime from the age of three to four months or older The sooner the dog is neutered, the less likely he will be to develop the hormones that give it those undesirable habits of leg-lifting on furniture, wandering away, and being overly interested in other dogs he meets.

5. **Consider your lifestyle.** We've already covered some major aspects of this, but there is one we must mention here.

If your job takes you out of town a great deal, have you thought about who will care for your dog when you're gone? I have a neighbor who is a recovery room nurse, subject to being called out for emergencies in the middle of the night. She loves dogs and has, in the past, owned several. But her work now demands so much of her time that she has chosen not to have a dog of her own. Instead, whenever she feels the need for some doggie attention, she visits my Poodle, Ginger. They snuggle and play together and when it's time to go back to the hospital, she never has to worry about who will care for a dog of her own.

If you travel, you'll have to make arrangements to board your dog. If you work excessively long hours, you must arrange to have someone come to your home and exercise and feed your friend. All this costs money and you need to think about this matter before you obtain a dog.

6. **In the case of a dog living in a family situation, who will be responsible for the care, feeding and training of the dog?** It should be someone who has the time and desire to be a caregiver,

A mixed breed will make a wonderful playmate for a child. A dog is also a great way to teach a child responsibility and respect for animals.

as well as the ability to physically manage the dog at all times.

Leaving such important matters to young children just isn't fair to the dog or the children. Your children may want to care for the dog, but are too young to handle the job. For instance, a five-year-old is not strong enough to exercise a large dog that can pull him down the street and cause havoc in the neighborhood, to say nothing of the physical danger to the child.

Dogs need to be trained. Are your children old enough to take the dog to obedience classes? Do they have the time and inclination to practice every day? An untrained dog is often cause for serious behavior problems and will, if not trained, become a burden rather than a joy in your life.

Housebreaking and training will be covered in detail. But for now, let this mention of it remind you

that if you're considering a puppy, it will be a major concern for several months. Young puppies need to go out often!

7. **Finally, if you have yet to bring a new dog into your home, have you prepared the home itself for the arrival of the dog?** If you've already welcomed a new dog, do you have the necessary conditions for the successful transition to your facility?

Successfully answering the questions in the preceding "Seven Steps to Sanity" can make the difference between havoc and happiness, so take the time now to familiarize yourself with them. Be assured it's never too late to organize life around the house so that you and your dog have the best chance possible to enjoy a winning relationship. An intelligent approach to dog ownership includes preparation, care, and commitment.

Penny, a Shih Tzu- Miniature Schnauzer mix, takes a ride in owner Judy Sicilia's car—wearing a safety harness of course!

MIXED BREED SOURCES

Shelters and Humane Societies

Every community has some form of animal rescue facility and most are run by caring people who try hard to find new homes for unwanted dogs. They get the dogs from people who no longer want or can care for a dog, from people whose dog produced a litter of unwanted puppies, dogs found wandering homeless, and occasionally from law enforcement people who removed the dog from an abusive situation.

Some of these dogs can be rehomed successfully and will make loving pets for their new adoptive families. Most will need some special attention to help them recover from the trauma of being uprooted from their original owners. A few may be so scarred by the transfer that they never recover and thus must be euthanized.

Adopting a mixed breed puppy directly out of its litter gives you the opportunity to study the entire

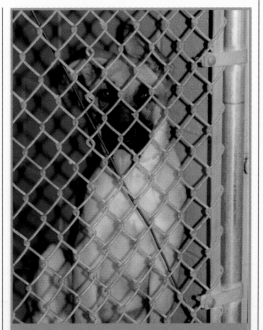
Most mixed breeds that are found in shelters can be successfully re-homed and, with the right owners and training, become loving pets.

litter and choose the individual you feel will best match your personality and lifestyle. Whether you get the puppy from a shelter or an individual owner, the folks you deal with will most likely show concern regarding how you intend to raise and care for their little puppy, so be prepared to talk freely with them and ask questions, too.

Every once in a while you may find an ad in the newspaper for a mixed breed dog. Sample phone calls in response to such ads revealed that, in most cases, the dogs were adults. Moving away, housing restrictions, allergies to dog hair, and most often, behavior problems were the reasons given for the owners' decisions to get rid of the dogs.

Shelters are wonderful places to get dogs—not only can you acquire a new best friend, you are saving a life!

As an obedience instructor for many years, I have found that frequently the unruly dog in one home can be transformed into the loving dog in another. All it takes is some training. It's a simple matter of understanding the dog's behavior, knowing how to train the dog, and taking the time to practice.

A perfect example of this is the famous TV dog known as "Eddie" on the show *Frasier.* That little terrier had two unsuccessful relationships before he was adopted into his present home. After training and loving patience, the current owner recognized his intelligence and willingness to perform and "Eddie" became a TV star.

Choosing a puppy versus an adult is another matter. If you have the time and patience to raise a puppy, the experience can be remarkable. Watching a dog grow into adulthood and develop his own personality is a fascinating experience.

You will have to get up early every morning and be available throughout the day for frequent trips to the puppy's elimination area. You'll need to serve several small meals a day according to the puppy's physical requirements. You'll have to teach him what is and what is not acceptable behavior, and see to his veterinary needs such as puppy shots, wormings, neutering, etc. But for all this effort, you'll be able to mold the little fellow into the kind of dog you'll enjoy for many years to come.

On the other hand, bringing an adult dog into your home skirts all those things, but you'll have to help the dog make the transition to your home, give him time to adjust to your lifestyle, and observe the dog carefully to discover what he does and doesn't like in the way of foods, play things, habits, exercise routines, and his ability to stay alone when you leave the house without him. For many people, adopting an adult dog is the closest thing to a ready-made friend they can get and the arrangement works well.

Whether you decide on a puppy or an adult, be sure the dog is healthy when you bring him home. A sickly dog is an expensive proposition and can take weeks, even months, to correct. Remember, no matter how cute and appealing the dog, getting a healthy dog will serve you both well in the future.

Moving into a new home with new people can be a stressful event for the dog. A sickly one may get even sicker when he's brought into an unfamiliar environment. So take the new dog to the veterinarian and ask for a physical check-up before you make that final decision. It may be the best money you've spent in years!

As you can see, selecting the right dog for you is an important and exciting event. It can make or break one of the most rewarding experiences of your life, so take the time to choose wisely. Then enjoy the results!

If you do not have the time or inclination to train a puppy, consider adopting an adult dog from a shelter or rescue organization.

MIXED BREED SUCCESS STORIES

As with so many other situations in life, you often hear about the failures but you rarely hear the success stories. The statement that announces "Mixed breed? You don't want a mixed breed. They're just wild curs," is all too common.

Unfortunately, the people who make statements like that have never heard about all the wonderful mixed breeds who share their lives with people. They've never heard about how mixed breeds as well as purebreds bring joy and fulfillment into the lives of their families and everyone they meet. Or about mixed breeds who do things that improve mankind's quality of life, such as hearing ear dogs for deaf people, assistance dogs who aid handicapped people, and guide dogs for the blind. These dogs are serious workers who are on duty to help their owners whenever they're needed. Many are mixed breeds who were rescued from animal shelters and put through months of intensive training before being placed with owners who needed them.

There are hundreds of therapy dogs who comfort the sick, the lonely, and the confused when they visit homes, schools and hospitals. And everyone of them makes life a little better for the people whose lives they touch.

As an obedience instructor and dog behavior consultant, I have an opportunity to work with hundreds of mixed breeds. Some (only a few) are hopeless and end up being euthanized. Most survive whatever life brought them before caring owners brought them into class where they learned to lived in harmony with their human rescuers. The majority develop into fully functioning members of their families and are dearly loved.

Dr. Susan Hamman and her mixed breed guardian angel, Gretal. Gretal saved Susan's life after Susan was struck by a hit-and-run driver.

These are the dogs I'm going to introduce you to in this chapter. I'm quite certain that once you've met them you'll feel good about your decision to live with a mixed breed.

First, I'd like you to meet Gretal Hamman of Fort Myers, Florida. Gretal was adopted as a puppy from the Humane Society in Louisville, Kentucky by Susan Hamman. At the time, Susan was a 24-year-old medical student at the University of Louisville School of Medicine. Gretal was a small Corgi-Collie type mixed breed.

They lived in a small apartment where Gretal kept Susan company through the long nights of studying. She also waited patiently alone when Susan had ten to twelve hour shifts at the hospital. But she never complained. Instead, she was just thrilled to see Susan coming through the door so they could take long walks together.

One night in June 1990, Susan took Gretal for a late night walk out in front of her apartment. They stopped on the grass under a street light as Gretal sniffed around.

Suddenly, out of the dark, a speeding car came around the bend and struck Susan throwing her to the ground and knocking her unconscious. As Susan fell, she released her hold on Gretal's lead. The dog was thrown away from Susan as the car sped off into the night. Six-month-old Gretal was the first to reach Susan's side. She sat licking her face and barking incessantly until someone came out of the

McTavish, an abandoned Cairn Terrier, has found a new home and loving owners through a rescue organization.

apartment building to investigate the noise.

When Susan's neighbor saw what had happened, he called an ambulance for Susan and took Gretal back to her apartment where she'd be safe. Susan suffered cuts and bruises and recovered completely.

Today, Dr. Hamman recalls the incident. Caring for her young son, Jack, and another mixed breed named Gretchen, Susan says, "Gretal saved my life. I was unconscious but I'll never forget that night. Perhaps it was Gretal's way of thanking me for loving her and giving her a good home."

Next, I'd like to introduce you to Tramp. She's a German Shepherd-Siberian Husky mixed breed about two years old. Her owner, Larry Gavin, didn't find her—Tramp found Larry and neither have been the same since.

One day while Larry was standing on the deck of his home in North Carolina, he looked down at the ground below the deck and saw a thin, shivering mixed-breed dog looking up at him. Larry called to her. Hesitant at first, the dog finally came up the steps to him.

She was timid yet willing to be friends, appeared to be extremely hungry and was obviously lost. Larry knew that people sometimes took unwanted dogs out into the country where they dumped the dogs off and drove away. He suspected this was the case with Tramp.

Following a good meal, and several hours of getting to know Larry and his family, Tramp was invited into the house to meet the Gavin's older dog, a Spitz. After some tentative moments, the two dogs accepted each other and Tramp began to settle in. Larry searched for Tramp's owner by placing an ad in the local paper. He went to the humane society, queried neighbors, put up notices in local shops. Nothing happened. Nobody claimed the lost dog so Larry named her Tramp and had her spayed. She was an official member of the Gavin family.

Now, a year later, Tramp and Larry have successfully completed a basic beginners obedience class and have moved up to an advanced training class. Tramp has become a happy, friendly pet. Most of all, Larry and Tramp have bonded together and the two

Larry Gavin teaches his German Shepherd-Siberian Husky mix Tramp to walk up the cat walk ramp. Lots of love, praise and affection have transformed Tramp into a model pet.

friends seem made for each other.

"She's the most wonderful dog I've ever had," comments Larry. "And she just loves everyone." Another happy ending to a sad beginning.

Lady also had a sad beginning but the end of her story is a triumphant one. This little terrier type mixed breed lives in St. James City, Florida with owner Peggy Harmon.

Two years ago, Lady was living with a family who didn't really care about her and refused to spend money to spay her. Consequently, she got pregnant and delivered a litter of puppies on Christmas day.

On December 27th, the family brought Lady and her litter to a local animal shelter, said they didn't want any of them, and drove away. Shelter employees took Lady and her family in and cared for them all.

When the puppies were about six weeks old, the local newspaper ran a picture of Lady as *Pet of the Week*. That's when Peggy saw Lady for the first time. It was love at first sight. Peggy, who lives alone, immediately went to the shelter and adopted Lady. The puppies went to new homes as well when they were about eight weeks old.

Soon Peggy and Lady were enrolled in an obedience class where Lady was taught manners and the two became a team. Today, Lady guards Peggy's home, fills Peggy's days with fun and activity, and worships Peggy's grandchildren.

Lady, a terrier-mix owned by Peggy Harmon, was dumped with her litter of two-day-old puppies at an animal shelter. Today Lady is spayed, all her puppies have been adopted and she is a valued and cherished member of the Harmon household.

Lady won't be having any more puppies, but that doesn't matter. What she does have is so much more valuable and rewarding than a hundred puppies could be; she shares a gift of love with Peggy every waking moment of every day. And Peggy returns that love to a little dog who brought fulfillment into her life.

Most mixed breeds originate from unwanted or unplanned breedings. Rarely do people deliberately unite two different breeds of dogs. What happens to the resulting unwanted offspring, however, is often a tragedy.

The puppies are dumped on lonely county roads, in shelters, or in shopping mall parking lots. They're turned loose to wander around until some kind soul picks them up and turns them in to animal shelters. Or worse, they're passed on to people who are ill prepared to raise and provide for a dog.

Occasionally, dogs are deliberately abused by emotionally disturbed individuals who derive pleasure from the animal's suffering. Such is the case of Ginger.

Neighbors in a small town in Florida kept hearing a soft plaintive whine but no one was able to locate the source of the cry. This went on for several days and the whimpering continued. Finally someone found a small puppy in a deep drainage culvert.

The puppy was laying in the dirt and didn't move when the person called down to the dog. When the Lee County Humane Society rescue team arrived, what they found was shocking. The puppy, about three months old, was wearing a plastic collar. Attached to the collar was a wire that wound around the collar and then down to the dog's hind foot. Thus the puppy was unable to walk or even move so she just lay there in the ditch and cried.

Back at the shelter, staff members cut away the wire, removed the collar and discovered that the wire had pierced through the puppy's flesh. In addition, the puppy was so traumatized, she hid under any piece of furniture she could find at the mere sight of a human being.

Pam Reilly, a shelter staff member, volunteered to work with the puppy. The first thing Pam did was to give the little creature a name. She called her Ginger for the light tan short coat. It was determined that Ginger was probably a mix of hound and sporting dog.

A month of fattening up Ginger followed. Next, Pam decided it was time to get Ginger some professional behavioral help. Only by working with her on a daily basis, Pam knew, would Ginger ever be suitable for adoption.

Pam and Ginger worked together for four months. Eventually Ginger came out from under the furniture and began trusting people again. Finally the behavior consultant suggested that Pam begin a search for just the right loving family for the now medium-sized dog.

Not long after, a family was found and Ginger ventured out into her new world. However, it wasn't successful. The adopting family had an older dog that absolutely refused to accept Ginger into the home. Ginger was returned to the shelter once again.

Pam immediately resumed working with Ginger. They went for rides in the shelter truck, to visit other employees in the shelter office, and for long walks where Ginger was encouraged to investigate her surroundings. Slowly, Ginger's self-confidence increased and luck came her way again.

A second family was found and Ginger went off with them to try one more time. This time in a home with no other pets, Ginger found love and care.

Now three years later, Ginger's wounds have healed, her traumatic beginnings are dull memories, and she lives a comfortable life with folks who love her. In exchange, she gives her family the love and devotion she was capable of giving when someone betrayed her.

Dogs, it seems, can be very forgiving. They can learn to trust their human companions and offer up their love and dedication in exchange for humane treatment. It usually doesn't take much to bring out the best in them.

Now that you're the owner of an All-American dog, you're about to discover that unique quality of trust and love your dog has for you. All you need do is be kind, gentle, loving and fair. The reward for you both is priceless. And one day when someone asks how you like your dog, you'll say, "He's the best dog I've ever had."

Bear is a mixed breed of German Shepherd-Airedale descent. He is very protective over home and family, yet will quickly befriend anyone his owner Claudia Mahaffey does.

FEEDING

If you obtain a dog from an animal shelter or previous owner, get a list of the brand and kind of food the dog has been eating. Dogs have very sensitive digestive systems and changing brands abruptly will usually cause diarrhea and great discomfort to the dog, to say nothing of the extra cleanup work for you.

environment and being separated from his former home is traumatic enough; he does not need physical stress added to that.

In the case of a puppy, you can expect he'll be eating three or four times a day. Thus, you'll need to make arrangements to continue that schedule for several more weeks.

Find out the brand or kind of dog food your puppy has been previously fed and stick to it.

Also find out how many meals a day the dog is getting. The times of day a dog eats are important, too, so be sure and get as many details about the dog's eating habits as possible. Does he eat dry, semi-moist, or canned food? What brands does he like?

Try to maintain this schedule for at least two weeks after you get him. Changing his

Water should also be available at all items during the day when he's out of his crate. At night, however, it's wise to restrict water consumption to a few sips after his last meal of the day. You and the dog will not want to get up too many times during the night!

Never feed a dog from your plate or the dinner table. This can become a very annoying habit and

Carrots are rich in fiber, carbohydrates and vitamin A. The CarrotBone™ by Nylabone® is a durable chew containing no plastics or artificial ingredients and can be served as-is, in a bone-hard form, or microwaved to a biscuit consistency.

one that's difficult to break once it's established. Dogs should eat dog food, not junk food. The major dog food manufacturers spend millions of dollars a year on researching the best diets for canines. Make use of this information and avoid feeding your dog foods that will not help him maintain good health or may cause stomach upset.

If and when you want to switch brands or types of dog food, talk to your veterinarian. He or she will suggest an appropriate diet and the amounts as well as number of meals per day that will most benefit your dog.

As a general rule, puppies between two and six months of age should be fed three meals a day. From six to twelve months, puppies should be given two meals a day. When the puppy reaches one year of age, you may feed him once or twice a day for life.

When selecting a dog food for your mixed breed, make sure it provides adequate nutrition and is appropriate for his stage of life.

I prefer to feed my adults twice a day. That way, I can feed smaller amounts that will not cause stomach bloating and the dogs seem to enjoy eating at the same time as my family does. After all, smelling food cooking in the kitchen stimulates their appetites as well as ours, so twice daily works for us.

Always feed your dog in the same place and never allow children to bother the dog while he's eating. I choose to feed my dogs in the kitchen. It's clean, near the area of preparation, free of insects that are attracted to bowls of food outdoors, and allows me an opportunity to observe how eagerly and how much each dog consumes.

Free feeding is an option whereby you place dry food in a bowl and just let the dog help himself whenever the mood strikes. This method, however, has several disadvantages.

First, you'll never know exactly how much and when a dog is eating. Secondly, food left out can spoil quickly in warm temperatures, thereby making your dog sick. And thirdly, you miss seeing any subtle hints that the dog is not feeling well when he nibbles half-heartedly.

By feeding on a regular schedule where you can observe the dog eating, you're able to monitor the dog's health and know exactly how he's feeling at any given time. Thus, when problems occur, this method draws your attention to the onset of trouble before it becomes serious.

When feeding both puppies and adults, put down the food bowl and leave it alone for 15 minutes. At the end of that time, remove the bowl and offer no more food until the next scheduled meal. Dogs quickly figure out that when the food bowl is presented, they'd better get right to it before you take it away. This leaves no chance for attracting unwanted pests in the kitchen or for developing picky eaters.

POPpups® are 100% edible and enhanced with dog-friendly ingredients like liver, cheese, spinach, chicken, carrots, or potatoes. They contain no sugar, salt, alcohol, plastic, or preservatives. You can even microwave a POPpup® to turn into a huge crackly treat.

GROOMING

Every dog needs to be groomed periodically. A long-coated dog will need to be brushed several times a week to keep the coat free of debris and knots. A short-coated dog should be brushed at least once a week.

Very young puppies have soft fluffy coats that give them that appealing cuddly appearance. As they grow, this soft coat begins to fall out and is replaced by an adult coat usually made up of a soft undercoat and a longer, stiffer type of hair that protects them from water and debris.

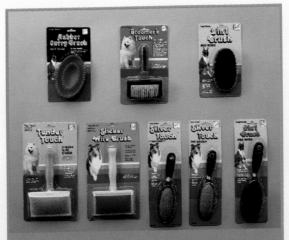

Four Paws offers an extensive line of grooming brushes, from slickers to curry brushes to pin brushes. These are sure to suit the grooming needs of every dog. Photo courtesy of Four Paws.

Proper brushing not only removes debris and loose hair, it serves to stimulate the skin which, in turn, helps to develop that healthy, clean shine a good coat must have.

Accepting the shedding process and keeping the dog well groomed will enable you to prevent fur balls around the house and discomfort to the dog. Finally, a regular schedule of grooming serves to build a close bond between dog and owner.

In the case of dogs who are obviously descended from Poodles, Bichon Frises, and other extensively groomed breeds, you may want to have the dog groomed professionally three or four times a year. Groomers can suggest styles of haircuts that will make your dog look his best and help you keep him looking nice all the time.

A medium-bristle brush is ideal for use on a dog with medium-length hair, while a hound glove is perfect for that short-coated dog. Brushes, combs and gloves can be found in most pet shops and animal supply stores. If you're not sure what type of tool you should use on your dog, ask your veterinarian.

Dirt caused by mud is easy to remove from a dog's coat. Simply allow the dirt to dry, then brush briskly until that desirable shine reappears in the coat. Bathing too often dries the skin and hair and causes an unattractive dullness.

Many veterinarians and professional dog handlers suggest

Available at pet shops today are grooming products that not only groom your dog but also remove any loose hair while massaging your pet. Photo courtesy of Four Paws.

immediately. Keep him out of drafts and cold air while he's drying or use a hair dryer on low heat to hasten the process.

During cold weather, do not allow the dog to go outdoors until he's thoroughly dry. A good brushing once the dog is dry will remove any remaining dead hair and stimulate the release of those precious skin oils for that healthy-coat look.

Two other matters of grooming must be mentioned here. Keeping your dog's teeth in good condition is essential for healthy gums. Your veterinarian will teach you how to clean your dog's teeth. He'll also suggest the best products to use for gum and teeth hygiene. There are a great variety of Nylabone® products available that veterinarians recommend as

bathing a dog no more than once every two to four weeks providing the dog is brushed regularly. Dogs that live outdoors and run in the rain need bathing even less often.

If the dog gets paint or tar-type substances on his coat, apply a liberal amount of mineral oil to the paint, let it soak in for a few minutes, then rub briskly with an absorbent cloth. Follow with a good bath. Stronger chemicals used to remove paints can cause burring and irritation to the skin, which later may require veterinary attention.

To bathe a dog, use a regular dog shampoo and warm water. Wet the dog down, apply shampoo and rub it into a lather, the same way you shampoo your own hair. Rinse thoroughly with warm water and towel dry the dog

A regular grooming regimen will not only make your mixed breed look better, but will also help you keep on top of any coat or skin problems your dog might experience.

safe and healthy for your dog to chew on.

Toenails must be trimmed and this, too, can be learned from your veterinarian. If you start when your dog is a puppy and teach him to sit still for nail trimming, you'll have no problem when he's an adult. However, some people wait until the dog is fully grown and by then, the dog hates nail trimming so he threatens to bite the trimmer. This is unacceptable behavior. At this point, the veterinarian will have to muzzle the dog for trimming and you'll have to pay for it. Make it economical for yourself and easy on the dog— teach nail trimming when the dog is young.

The puppy you choose should welcome your attention and affection and be curious about the world around him.

Dental products are available for helping to fight plaque, reduce tartar build-up and control unpleasant breath in dogs. Photo courtesy of Four Paws.

EXERCISE

Exercising for muscle building and coordination skills, for fun and bonding, and for learning are all important aspects of helping your new dog become a great companion.

Muscle building and coordination skills can be developed in the very young puppy with simple games of fetch played indoors. Since his bones are not fully grown and hardened, excessive exercising is dangerous and may cause physical problems later in life.

For the eight-week-old puppy, just following you around the kitchen and family room will soon tire him out and he'll collapse into a deep sleep for anywhere from ten to thirty minutes. As the puppy grows, his capacity for exercise will increase and you'll see his need for more and more exercise grow with him.

Taking the puppy to different environments such as a shopping center, park, beach, or a wooded trail not only serves to socialize the puppy but gives him plenty of exercise to strengthen his developing muscles. In addition, it serves to help you and the puppy

Most puppies love to play and thrive with plenty of fun and exercise.

build a strong bond of loyalty to each other.

For puppies twenty weeks of age and older as well as adult dogs, exercising as a form of learning brings great pleasure to both teacher (you) and student (dog). Teach the dog to walk a "plank" to build his self-confidence while strengthening leg muscles as he walks along and tries not to fall off. Use the bench seat of a picnic table or a narrow cement curb along a driveway. Always keep one hand on the dog to prevent falls, assure him that all is well and praise lavishly when he reaches the end. Soon he'll begin to think he's a great athlete!

Find other ways around your home to build muscle, heart and stamina in your dog. Use lots of praise, even a food treat, to demonstrate to the dog your pride in his efforts. Remember, a strong dog is a healthy dog and one that's at ease wit himself and his abilities to cope with life.

PLAY AND TOYS

Playing with safe toys is excellent exercise for your dog, as well as very rewarding for the both of you. There are some toys that the dog can use alone and others that are more fun when you play, too.

A Gumabone Frisbee™ is an exciting disc that you fling through the air and the dog can learn to run and jump up to catch mid-air. Tossing a Chooz™ or a Nylabone® for the dog to retrieve provides chewing satisfaction as well as muscle-building exercise. And the perennial favorite, a tennis ball, is always attractive because it keeps moving once it hits the ground.

Play hide-and-seek with your dog in a fenced yard. It's a fun game, builds strength and stamina and teaches one very important lesson. He learns to come to you when you call and enjoys the positive outcome

Mixed breeds can participate in agility trials. Agility exercises strengthen your dog's muscles while improving his coordination.

Playing with toys like the Nylabone® Frisbee® will not only keep your All-American in shape, but with keep his teeth healthy while he chews.

Make sure your dog always has plenty of cool, clean water available, especially after playing or exercising outside.

because he's praised and given a treat when he finds you. Later in life when you work on a more formal "Come," he'll remember the game and come enthusiastically.

Providing your dog gets along with other dogs, give him opportunities to play with other dogs under your supervision. Play fighting, play hunting, play stalking, play grooming, and power playing are nature's way of teaching your dog how to conduct himself peacefully with other dogs.

Aside from developing muscles and strength, playing with you is extremely beneficial to the bond you and the dog build together. Playing reinforces the idea that he is most certainly a vital member of your pack.

When you control the games—begin and end the games at your discretion, not the dog's—it sends a strong message to the dog that you are indeed the pack leader. That in itself teaches him to respect you, and makes learning other behaviors more successful and meaningful.

One word of caution, however, Always supervise the activity when dogs are playing with children. Both can get carried away with excitement and forget to control their behavior. Keep it peaceful and not physically harmful.

THE ACTIVE MIXED BREED

Not all mixed breeds go from a loving birth environment into the arms of equally caring homes. Some have traumatic beginnings. Perhaps the road to your front door was a long, often bumpy one, for the dog, one filled with frightening experiences, even turbulent and painful ones.

However, once you've decided a particular dog is the one you want to live with, you can help him see another kind of person. A gentler, kinder, more caring human being. And, being a dog, he'll probably be willing to try one more time to co-habitate with a human.

He'll adapt to your lifestyle and learn to respect you as the leader of his pack who exercises fairness, yet firmness. What's more, he may even learn to do all manners of fun and exciting things with you if you enjoy being with him as much as he enjoys being with you.

Let's look at some of the possibilities for the future. He can learn to help you around the home and yard by fetching things such as the newspaper, the mail, tools, his own lead, and toys. Some dogs even go to work with their owners every day.

Most dogs love learning tricks and your dog will be no different if you lavish him with praise when he succeeds at the smallest of attempts. And playing games with him will always bring a

Sly, a Sheltie mix owned by Sharon Drescosky, shows his athleticism by flying over the bar jump.

resounding "Yeah!" when you show him that a fun and game session is coming. There are many books of tricks and games you can use.

Agility training is offered by many dog training clubs. This activity helps to turn the flabbiest house pet into a well-muscled athlete who loves to run, climb, crawl, and jump. Look into an agility club in your area by contacting kennel clubs, veterinarians, or obedience minutes or hours before. In tracking, the dog uses his astonishing scenting ability to show you where a person went. The most difficult thing about tracking is that you must learn to trust your dog's nose and follow him. If taught correctly, he'll lead you right to the person or an article that the "lost" person dropped along the way. Once bitten by the tracking bug, you may want to get serious about it and enter tracking trials. When

Larry Gavin teaches Tramp to go through a tunnel with the promise of a food treat when she accomplishes her goal.

instructors. Obedience competition is challenging and rewarding for those who succeed. Call a local training club to see what's available to you and your dog.

Tracking is a fascinating hobby for both of you. Teaching a dog to track means he learns to use his nose to follow the path of a person who has gone ahead of him the dog passes the tracking tests, he'll be awarded a Tracking Dog title by the sponsoring organization.

Next, think about all you and your dog can do outdoors together. Try hiking in the woods, swimming, boating, camping, jogging, bicycling, and playing fetch together. All of these sports are attractive to normal, healthy

Suzie, a Labrador mix with plenty of enthusiasm, has been trained by owner Cheri VanDeGejuchte in basic obedience.

go into homes for the aged to bring a few brief moments of joy to otherwise lonely people.

Seeing the joy on the faces of the people whose lives Therapy dogs touch is worth more than words can describe. And knowing that you'll go back another day to repeat the gift of love offered by the dog will be reward enough for you.

For a dog to become a Therapy Dog, he must have a calm, stable temperament, love people and traveling, and be unmoved by unusual activities such as wheelchairs rolling down a hall, a person on crutches or a walker, or children hooked up to tubes and machines that hum.

The American Kennel Club offers a Canine Good Citizen certificate to dogs who can demonstrate their ability to be well-mannered under a variety of circumstances. There are often classes and tests for CGC certification offered in many communities around the country. If you're interested in having your dog earn a Canine Good Citizen certificate, contact local training clubs and obedience schools for more information or write to the American Kennel Club at 51 Madison Avenue, New York, NY 10010. The Mixed Breed Dog Club of America can also help you get started. In addition, they can tell you about other activities organized for mixed breeds in your locality. Their address is 100 Acacia Ave., San Bruno, CA, 94066.

Therapy Dogs International is another organization that will test

dogs, especially when they can do them with the person they love.

If you're a family person, these are the same activities children of all ages find most appealing. When you urge the family to get involved with you and the dog, you'll be helping to build healthy humans as well. What a bonus that is!

Finally, I'd like you to consider therapy work for your dog. This is one of the most rewarding and generous activities your dog can perform in life. Therapy dogs visit hospitals to cheer up sick children and elderly people. They go to schools to demonstrate how well-mannered dogs behave. They your dog's stability and willingness to be among other dogs and people. Upon passing the test, the TDI will register you and your dog as a Therapy Dog team. For more information, contact them at 6 Hilltop Rd., Mendham, NJ 07945.

Whatever activity catches your imagination, your dog will learn to love it providing you train him well and reward him generously for a job well done. Even the littlest dog needs to feel special, so don't allow your new dog to become a couch potato. Make his life as exciting and fulfilled as yours.

Your chosen activity can be something your dog does every day or something he does on weekends and holidays only. As long as he can do things with you, his greatest need will be satisfied. Remember that all dogs, mixed breeds and purebreds alike, want and need to live and work with human beings.

Mixed breeds can also be trained as service dogs. This Golden-Lab mix is a Seeing Eye dog.

HOUSEBREAKING YOUR MIXED BREED

Let's discuss housing and housebreaking your dog. Most people today want their dogs to live indoors with them. Only in rare cases, usually people who own large properties or farms, do dogs live out-of-doors.

The dog will need a sleeping place that is his own and that provides a place of security for him while you're away from the home and at night. He'll also need a place where he can rest quietly while you're busy around the house.

For puppies, the best and safest way is to crate train him as early in life as possible. Crates can be made of wire or fiberglass and can be purchased in many different sizes to fit individual dogs. Just be sure it's large enough for him to lay down and stretch out or stand up and not bump his head on the top of the crate.

Initially, an old towel placed on the floor of the crate will provide comfort to the dog. Once you're sure he won't chew up the

Your All-American will look to you, his owner, to give him the guidance and discipline he needs to be accepted in your family.

bedding, you can graduate to fancier cushions or pillows.

Older dogs who have previously been crate trained should be given a crate in your home. They will recognize this place as being familiar and it will greatly enhance their ability to make a speedy adjustment to your home.

Older dogs who have never been crate trained will need to be taught to use one. For them, I suggest treating them exactly as if they were puppies and following the six steps for crate training. Patience and reassurance are important for these dogs and once they learn that being in a crate is safe, they'll enjoy their new "cubby."

Resting places are for times when you're around the house and the dog wants to nap or play quietly with a toy or chew on a bone. The place can be a small rug or bean bag bed or other commercial-type soft bed that is set in a family room or kitchen area. As long as the dog can see and hear you, his resting space will help keep him from underfoot during times of high family traffic and meal preparation.

Puppies, however, often use the resting space rug or bed as a chew toy itself, so this item should be reserved for when he is no longer teething on anything he can get his mouth around.

To crate train a dog, whether it's a puppy or older dog, use the following method for success in the least amount of time. Don't skip any of the steps and be willing to go back to an earlier step if the dog has difficulty with any of the stages.

In addition to keeping your dog and your possessions safe from destruction, crate training is the easiest way to housebreak a dog, whether it be a puppy or an adult that simply isn't reliably trained. This is what I call my "Success Method." It is designed to give you, the owner, a simple yet effective way to help your dog develop clean living habits and a feeling of security in his new environment. (Note: I use the term "puppy." However, this applies to adult dogs in housetraining as well.)

TYPES OF HOUSETRAINING

You can train a puppy to relieve itself wherever you choose. For example, city dwellers often train their puppies to relieve themselves in the gutter because large plots of grass are not readily available. Suburbanites, on the other hand, usually have yards to accommodate their dogs' needs.

Outdoor training includes such surfaces as grass, dirt, and cement. Indoor training usually means training a dog to newspaper or a paper-lined litter pan (appropriate for small and toy breeds).

When deciding on the surface and location that you'll want your dog to use, be sure it's going to be permanent. Training a dog to grass and then changing your mind two months later is extremely difficult for both dog and owner.

Next, choose the command you'll use each and every time you want your puppy to void. "Go hurry up" and "Go make" are examples of commands commonly used by dog owners.

Get in the habit of asking the puppy, "Do you want to go hurry up?" (or whatever your chosen relief command is) before you take him out. That way, when he becomes an adult, you'll be able to determine if he wants to go out when you ask him. A confirmation will be signs of interest, wagging his tail, watching you intently, going to the door, etc.

Most of all, be consistent. Always take your dog to the same location, always use the same command, and always have him on lead when he's in his relief area.

By following the "Success Method," your puppy will be completely housetrained by the time his muscle and brain development reach maturity. Keep in mind that small breeds usually mature faster than large breeds, but all puppies should be trained by six months of age.

Your puppy needs to relieve himself after play periods, after each meal, after he's been sleeping, and any time he indicates he's looking for a place to urinate or defecate.

The urinary and intestinal tract muscles of very young puppies are not fully developed. Therefore, like human babies, puppies need to relieve themselves frequently.

Take your puppy out often—every hour for an eight-week-old, for example. The older the puppy, the less often he'll need to relieve himself. Finally, as a mature, healthy adult, he'll require only three to five relief trips per day.

CRATE TRAINING

Since the type of housing and control you provide for your puppy has a direct relationship on the success of housetraining, we should consider the various aspects of both before we begin training.

Bringing a new puppy home and turning him loose in you house can be compared to turning a child loose in a sports arena and telling the child the place is all his. The sheer enormity of the place would be too much for him to handle.

Instead, offer the puppy clearly

Take your puppy out often to lessen the chances of accidents in the home. Jake, a five-month-old Labrador mix owned by Bill Burdine, enjoys a walk.

defined areas where he can play, sleep, eat, and live. A room of the house where the family gathers the most is the obvious choice. Puppies are social animals and need to feel a part of the pack right from the start. Hearing your voice, watching you while you're doing things, or smelling you nearby are all positive reinforcers that he is now a member of your pack. Usually a family room, the kitchen, or a nearby adjoining breakfast nook is ideal for providing safety and security for both puppy and owner.

Within that room, there should be a smaller area that the puppy can call his own. A cubby hole, a wire or fiberglass dog crate, or a fenced (not boarded!) corner from which he can view the activities of his new family will be fine.

The size of the crate is the key factor here. The area must be large enough for the puppy to lay down and stretch out, as well as stand up without rubbing his head on the top, yet small enough so that he cannot relive himself at one end and sleep at the other without coming into contact with his droppings.

Dogs are, by nature, clean

animals and will not remain close to their relief areas unless forced to do so. In those cases, they then become dirty dogs and usually remain that way for life.

By providing sleeping and resting quarters that fit the dog, and offering frequent opportunities to relieve himself outside his quarters, the puppy quickly learns that the outdoors (or the newspaper if you're training him to paper) is the place to go when he needs to urinate or defecate. It also reinforces his innate desire to keep his sleeping quarters clean. This, in turn, helps develop the control muscles that will eventually produce a dog with clean living habits.

The crate should be lined with a clean towel and offer one toy, no more. Do not put food or water in the crate, as eating and drinking will activate his digestive processes and ultimately defeat your purpose, as well as make the puppy very uncomfortable as he attempts to "hold it."

Never line his sleeping area with newspaper. Puppy litters are usually raised on newspaper and, once in your home, the puppy will immediately associate newspaper with voiding. Never put newspaper on any floor while house training as this will only confuse the puppy. If you're paper training him, use paper in his designated relief area ONLY. Finally, restrict water intake after evening meals. Offer a few licks at a time—never let a young puppy gulp water after meals.

One method of housebreaking is paper training. Teach your puppy to relieve himself on newspapers, then place the papers closer and closer to the door.

CONTROL

By control, we mean helping the puppy to create a lifestyle pattern that will be compatible to that of his human pack. Just as we guide little children to learn our way of life, we must show the puppy when it's time to play, eat, sleep, exercise, even entertain himself.

Your puppy should always sleep in his crate. He should also learn that, during times of household confusion and excessive human activity, such as at breakfast when family members are preparing for the day, he can play by himself in relative safety and comfort in his crate. Each time you leave the puppy alone, he should be crated. Puppies are chewers. They can't tell the difference between lamp cords, television wires, shoes, table legs, etc. Chewing into a television wire, for example, can be fatal to the puppy, while a shorted wire can start a fire in the house.

If the puppy chews on the arm of a chair when he's alone, you'll probably discipline him angrily when you get home. Thus, he makes the association that your coming home means he's going to be hit or punished. (He won't remember chewing up the chair and is incapable of making the association of the discipline with his naughty deed.)

If you have a small child in the home who wants to get into the puppy's food bowl every time he eats, feeding the pup in his crate is the answer. The child can't disturb the dog, and the pup will be free to eat in peace.

Other times of excitement such as family parties, etc. can be fun for the puppy, providing he can view the activities from the security of his crate. He's not underfoot, he's not being fed all sorts of tidbits that will probably

Putting your mixed breed on feeding schedule will help to regulate the times he will need to go out.

If you take your puppy to the same place to eliminate, he will soon know what is expected of him.

cause him stomach distress, yet he still feels a part of the fun.

SCHEDULE

As stated earlier, a puppy should be taken to his relief area each time he's released from his crate, after meals, after a play session, when he first awakens in the morning (at eight weeks, this can mean five in the morning!), and whenever he indicates by circling or sniffing busily that he needs to urinate or defecate. For puppies under ten weeks of age, a routine of taking him out every hour is necessary. As the puppy grows, he'll be able to wait for longer periods of time.

Keep trips to his relief area short. Stay no more than five or six minutes and then return to the house. If he goes during that time, praise lavishly and take him indoors immediately. If he doesn't, but he has an accident when you go back indoors, pick him up immediately, say "No! No!" and return to his relief area. Wait a few minutes, then return to the house

All dogs should have regular play and exercise times with members of their family. This All-American takes a walk on the beach.

can include fetching games with a large ball or an old sock with a knot tied in the middle. (All puppies teeth and need soft things on which to chew.) Remember to restrict play periods to indoors within his living area (the family room, for example) until he's completely housetrained.

Let the puppy learn that going outdoors means it's time to relieve himself, not play. Once trained, he'll be able to play indoors and out and still differentiate the times for play versus the times for relief.

Help him develop regular hours for naps, being alone, playing by himself and just resting, all in his crate. Encourage him to entertain himself while you're busy with your activities. Let him learn that having you near is comforting, but your main purpose in life is not to

Crate training is the easiest and least stressful way to housebreak your All-American.

again. NEVER hit a puppy or rub his face in urine or excrement when he has an accident!

Once indoors, put him in his crate until you've had time to clean up his accident. Then release him to the family area and watch him more closely than before. Chances are, his accident was a result of your not picking up his signal or waiting too long before offering him the opportunity to relieve himself. NEVER hold a grudge against the puppy for accidents.

The puppy should also have regular play and exercise sessions when he's with you or a family member. Exercise for a very young puppy can consist of a short walk around the house or yard. Playing provide him with undivided attention.

Each time you put the puppy in his crate, tell him "It's cubby time!" (or whatever command you choose). Soon, he'll run to his crate when he hears you say those words.

In the beginning of his training, don't leave him in his crate for prolonged periods of time, except during the night when everyone is sleeping. Make his experience with his crate a pleasant one and, as an adult, he'll love it and willingly stay in it for several hours. (There are millions of people who go to work every day and leave their adult dogs crated while they're away. The dogs accept this as their lifestyle and look forward to "crate time.")

Crate training provides safety for you, the puppy and the home.

It also provides the puppy with a feeling of security, and that helps develop a puppy with self-confidence and clean habits.

SIX STEPS TO SUCCESSFUL CRATE TRAINING

Remember, one of the primary ingredients in housetraining your puppy is control. And regardless of your lifestyle, there will always be occasions when you'll need to have a place where your dog can stay and be happy and safe. Crate training is the answer for now and in the future.

Below are the step-by-step directions to actually training your puppy to accept his crate as his den, a place of security and comfort. Follow each step in order and don't try to rush the final steps. A conscientious approach to training now will result in a happy

Most puppies will have to relieve themselves after eating, drinking, sleeping, or strenuous play. Be aware of the signs that your pup needs to go outside.

dog that willingly accepts your lifestyle as his own.

1. Tell the puppy, "it's cubby time!" and place him in the crate with a small treat (a piece of cheese or half a biscuit). Let him stay in the crate for five minutes while you are in the same room. Then release him and praise lavishly. Never release him when he's fussing. Wait until he's quiet before you let him out.

2. Repeat step one several times a day.

3. The next day, place the puppy in the crate as before. Let him stay there for ten minutes. Do this several times a day.

4. Continue building time in five minute increments until the puppy will stay in his crate for 30 minutes with you in the room. Always take him to his relief area after prolonged periods in his crate.

5. Now go back to the beginning and let puppy stay in his crate for five minutes while you are out of the room.

6. Once again build crate time in five minutes increments with you out of the room. When puppy will stay willingly in his crate (he may even fall asleep!) for 30 minutes with you out of the room, he'll be ready to stay in it for several hours at a time.

A few key elements are really all you need for a successful house and crate training method: consistency, frequency, praise, control, and supervision. By following these procedures with a normal, healthy puppy, you and the puppy will soon be past the stage of "accidents" and ready to move on to a full and rewarding life together.

Repetition may be boring for your puppy, but consistency is the key to housebreaking your mixed breed.

TRAINING YOUR MIXED BREED

Training a dog means many things to many people. It can mean teaching your dog a few simple commands to facilitate living with him and making your lives together harmonious. It can also mean giving your dog obedience lessons in a formal can do with their dogs, things like retriever field trails, sled pulling and teaching your dog to be a home helper who carries items around the house for you or brings you tools when you're doing chores. However, the behaviors discussed in my book

This Beagle-Basset mix is being trained to wear his collar and leash, not only for his safety, but for the safety of others as well.

class, then going on to teach him a dozen or more other behaviors that can consume the rest of your lives together. Things such as earning American Kennel Club obedience titles for purebreds or United Kennel Club titles for mixed breeds.

In my book, *Training Your Dog For Sports and Other Activities*, I present 30 different things people do not include such things as teaching your dog to rest quietly while the family is at the dinner table or not jumping on folks when they come to visit. A minimum level of control must be achieved before you can begin teaching your dog various sports activities.

It's easy to see, then, that a mere chapter on training must be

Teaching your dog to sit is one of the first training commands you will both try to master.

very limited in its scope. Remember there are dozens of books you can purchase that will help you teach your dog many disciplines. This chapter addresses some very basic control behaviors so you two can survive the initial period before you get into an obedience class.

Probably the most common and the easiest behavior we all teach our dogs is to sit on command. The trouble with many people is they don't really know how to do it successfully, so they nag the dog to death with "Sit, Sit, Sit, Siittt!"

When you give more than one command for a behavior — in other words you keep repeating the command over and over — you're only teaching the dog to count! By consistently nagging him with repeated commands for any behavior, the dog learns to wait until the pitch of your voice reaches the panic level before he obeys.

Instead, give a command ONE TIME ONLY and then help the dog perform the matching behavior. The second he succeeds, reward him with lots of praise and a food treat such as a piece of cheese or chicken or a soft biscuit.

Four Paws Quick Fit Muzzles are the most comfortable and humane muzzles for dogs. They allow dogs to drink water while wearing them and are made of nylon and are completely washable.

SIT

For example, let's see how that "Sit" command works. Find out before you begin what kind of treats your dog really likes best. Is it sharp cheddar cheese? A slice of hot dog? A chunk of steak? A bit of apple? Don't consider dry dog biscuits as it will take the dog to long to chew it up before he realizes the reward for the desired behavior.

Next take a treat and place it between your thumb and your first finger with the palm of your hand facing the dog so he can see the treat. Now lower your food hand to the dog's nose and let him lick the treat. As soon as he recognizes that you've got a treat in your hand, slowly raise the treat up over his head and back toward his tail. Keep the treat close to his mouth so he can lick it but not eat it.

As you begin moving your hand upward, say "Sit" once. He should focus his attention on the food as it moves. His nose will follow the movement of the food and when the food hand gets directly above his head, his nose will be facing the ceiling. At this point, his knees will bend as he adjusts his balance to the movement of his head rolling back and his nose pointing upward. When his knees bend, he'll assume the sit position without you ever actually touching him.

Whenever possible, manipulate the dog into a desired position. By physically forcing the dog into a certain position, you give him the opportunity to resist you. That's something you don't want the dog to learn—that he can resist.

Manipulating the dog into a

Basic obedience training will produce a well-mannered dog that will behave in any situation. Dustin Draffen with his mixed breed friend.

desired position and then praising him lavishly for doing it will help him learn the behavior quickly. Furthermore, he'll be anxious to repeat the behavior in order to earn more praise and treats. In other words, let the dog think he performed the behavior all by himself!

As soon as the dog sits, give him the treat and praise him like he'd just performed a miracle. Saying "Good boy" in a dull monotone just won't cut it with him. Clap your hands in applause. Celebrate with GOOD BOY!! You're so smart. What a fine chap you are (or whatever comes to your mind at the moment). Whatever you say, say it with gusto in an excited tone of voice.

If you want the dog to learn to sit on command and do it without hesitation for the rest of his life, you've got to make a big deal out of it during the learning process. Whenever I teach a dog a behavior and he begins to perform it (at that point, I'm usually helping him to do it), I tell him he's brilliant, a super dog, the smartest dog I've ever known. I praise convincingly and the dog responds to my enthusiasm. That's what makes him eager to try again.

The best method for success is one that produces a feeling of self confidence in the student. By feeling good about himself, the student thinks, "I can do this. I'm going to do it again in order to get some more praise and treats. I like what happened when I did it."

Sometimes when teaching the sit to very small puppies or toy breed dogs, the dog won't sit.

Instead, he'll begin to back up slowly away from you as he attempts to follow the food hand. If this happens, there's an easy way to help the dog understand what you want.

Have the food treat in your right hand and place it at the dog's nose as above. Now take the left hand and bend the fingers slightly to form a saucer shape. Place the saucer/hand gently against the dog's rump (the area from the base of his tail to just above his knees or stifle).

Now as you lift the food treat up over his head allowing the puppy to back up into your left hand, he'll slide into a sit position. You'll only have to do this a few times and the dog will get the idea that sitting means placing his rump the floor. Praise and treat immediately and simultaneously with great enthusiasm.

With either method, the dog will get the idea that the sound (remember, your dog does not speak English and, to him, your words are only sounds) "Sit" means to assume a sit position, for which he'll be handsomely rewarded. Shortly the dog will speed up his response to the command in order to hasten the subsequent rewards of food and praise.

Repeat this training method for several weeks on a daily basis and shortly you'll find that you can reward with food occasionally rather than every time, providing you always give him sincere verbal praise. Soon the food treats will no longer be necessary. He'll be happy with praise alone.

Sometimes when a dog doesn't accomplish a desired behavior, the problem lies not with the dog but with the owner's handling of the dog during the teaching process. For example, if your dog sits but then immediately jumps up, sits again, jumps again, the cause of this erratic behavior could be in your food hand. Do the exercise again and this time watch your food hand. Is it right at your dog's nose the entire time or are you moving your hand up and down in an attempt to prevent him from grabbing the treat? This is a very common mistake made by owners, so watch how you handle the dog. Chances are you're doing something that makes him behave the way he does.

The sit command is a control exercise and one of the most practical behaviors you can teach your dog. Since it's easy for you to teach and the dog to learn, it should be introduced as soon as possible after you get your dog. Once learned, it should become part of the dog's regular vocabulary and repertoire of behaviors.

SIT-STAY

Having succeeded at getting

Training your dog to stay will enable you to trust your dog to keep out of mischief if you must leave him for a short time. Two-month-old Wayah, owned by Lynne Coris.

some control you're now ready to get even more control with an equally simple behavior, the "stay." Stay means "You stay where you are. I'm going to leave you and I'll be right back." Once your dog learns that lesson, you'll really have control.

Think how much easier life will be for you when you can tell your dog to stay as you go do something and come back to him. For example, you open the front door, tell the dog to sit and stay in the doorway, and you go get the mail from the mailbox. Instead of racing out of the house and running through the streets, the dog waits patiently in the doorway and is there when you return with the mail. No more mad dash to catch a fleeing dog, no danger of the dog being hit by a car, no frantic chase around the neighborhood. Solution: Control!

To teach the stay, the dog needs to be wearing a simple buckle type collar and a leash or "lead" as we call it in training. A word here about leashes, or leads, before we get started. They are readily available from most pet shops in three to six foot lengths. Then, there's the retractable lead that stretches out for up to 16 feet.

The retractable lead is a wonderful invention because it allows your dog the freedom of wandering up to 16 feet away from you while you maintain control of him at the same time. It gives the dog permission to look around, sniff things on the ground, eliminate at a distance from you, and explore his territory to get out there ahead of you and pull hard. Therefore, the further he gets away from you, the more uncontrollable he becomes.

For the purposes of teaching control exercises, I recommend using either a four or six foot lead. Once the dog learns a behavior, he can be given freedom at further distances until he's finally reliable with no lead at all. Then, he's ready to use a retractable lead

When your dog can walk on lead without pulling, you can take him anywhere you want to go. These guys are enjoying a day in the park.

as you two stroll along.

However, I don't recommend using a retractable lead on a dog who has not yet learned to walk calmly beside you without pulling. When a small dog pulls the owner, he simply puts a bit of pressure on your arm. When a big dog pulls, he can pull you flat on your face in a split second and at the least he can cause muscle strain in your arm and shoulder. What's even worse about an untrained dog using a retractable lead is that he's being conditioned without treating you like you're a sled that he's determined to pull to Alaska!

Now hold the lead in your left hand and a treat in your right hand just as you did for teaching the sit. Tell the dog to sit and when he does, immediately go to stand beside him so that the dog is on your left side. Place your food hand at the dog's nose, let him lick the treat but don't let him eat it just yet.

As you stand beside the sitting dog and he's licking the treat, say "stay." Maintain that position for ten seconds then give him the treat and say "OK good boy. Good Fido."

The purpose of this step is to get the dog used to sitting still for short periods of time. No sitting and then quickly popping up again. He must learn to settle down and wait for your release command, "OK."

Repeat this sitting beside you quietly for several days. Using the food treat at the dog's nose will help him to focus his attention on you and maintain a sitting position for longer periods of time.

About the third day, we'll change things a bit. Now, immediately after you say "Stay," step out on your right foot to pivot directly in front of your dog so that you're standing facing him toe to toe. Your food hand is still at his nose and he's still sitting there watching the food.

Once you're directly in front of the dog, count to five and immediately return to the dog's side. Now, release him with "OK, good boy," praise and food. Once he has the "OK," he quickly learns that he's free to get up and enjoy the celebration of his success with you.

Often I see people trying to teach a dog to stay by moving away from the dog too soon. The dog doesn't understand what the owner wants so he gets up to follow. The owner then yells and punishes the dog for moving so the dog becomes even more confused.

By doing a sit-stay with you up close to the dog and your food

hand on his nose for several weeks, the dog becomes conditioned to sitting still while you are away from his side. Furthermore, being close to him helps you to keep him sitting as he learns that you're not going far away and you'll come right back to him. He looks forward to the resulting celebration.

Another mistake often made by owners is that food hand position again. If you stand in front of your dog waving the food hand around

If you begin training your mixed breed puppy early, he will soon become a valued friend and family member.

in any direction, the dog will probably get up. When this happens, you think the dog isn't getting the idea and learning to stay. The truth of the matter is that he's doing exactly what your hand is telling him to do—follow the food. Again the food hand *must* remain motionless at his nose from the moment you say "stay" until you return to his side when the exercise is over and you release him with that now-familiar "OK, good boy."

Once the dog is conditioned to sitting still while you stand out in front of him, he'll be able to do a sit-stay with you standing three feet away. Of course you must continue the celebration upon your return to his side, regardless of how far away you go from him.

The close up sit-stay should be used for several weeks before you attempt to move farther away while he's sitting still. Once you begin to move away from the dog, you must stop having food in your hand or the dog will, indeed, get up to follow the treat. However, by that time you can place his treat on a nearby table or chair and give it to him after you've returned to his side and verbally praised him. (That's how conditioning works: Instead of receiving the food as you praise him, he must now wait until the two of you get over to the table to fetch the treat. In other words, he's being conditioned to stay on command while he's always praised immediately yet the food treat takes longer to get until finally there's no food treat needed at all. This is the process of weaning off the food in training and, providing you always praise him for a good job, he'll be happy and willing to do it again.)

If the dog breaks from the sit position at any time during the various phases of teaching the sit-stay, don't get upset. Be patient and don't give up in frustration.

Re-sit the dog, tell him "No, sit" and resume the position you were in when he broke. Keep the stay portion of the exercise short initially. Remember the dog doesn't know what you want so,

by taking short, easy steps, he'll begin to see a pattern here of you leaving and returning, that is always followed by your praise.

Most dogs are very eager to please their masters. They need only to learn what you want and they'll try to comply. Never correct a dog for a failed exercise during the teaching phase. It isn't productive or fair to reprimand a dog for not doing something that he doesn't understand. Be patient!

If you practice daily and with patience, and always give sincere praise for his smallest achievements, the dog will learn in no time to be reliable when you say "stay." Best of all, he'll continue to do it for the rest of his life. Certainly the investment of a few weeks when you first get your dog will pay big dividends later on. And the bond you two build through working together will be lifelong as well.

To wean off the food treats, give a treat every other time he does a sit-stay, then every third time. Finally you can vary the occasions when food is given providing you never let the dog know when he's going to get a treat. Praise will always be important, so never fail to praise when he obeys your commands. Praise is the dog's pay for a job well done. Furthermore, he'll always look for your approval.

RECALL
Now let's talk about the behavior most dog owners want more than any other, teaching the dog to come when he's called.

Often times, this is also the behavior most difficult to teach and the most frustrating for the owner. However, I've found a way to teach coming when called and I've never seen a dog that didn't respond enthusiastically to it.

Normally when a person teaches a dog to come when he's called, the person uses the command "come." Too often this word is spoken in a short, guttural manner that sounds more like a threat than a promise, more like a Marine sergeant shouting orders to his troops.

"Come, Get over here!" are all too common commands we hear every day in training classes. And in the majority of cases, the dogs hearing those commands either flatly refuse to obey or attempt to run away. But can you blame them?

If I heard you command me to come in the manner used most often by dog owners, I'd run away, too, simply because the tone of voice promises trouble when I get to you. I want to be loved and praised when I get to you, not punished or physically disciplined.

The next big error made by owners is what follows once the dog refuses to come or heads in the opposite direction. The owner finally catches the dog and proceeds to "correct" such naughty behavior by yelling, jerking, even hitting the dog. Well, if that doesn't convince the dog that he doesn't want to go to his owner, I don't know what will.

Now let me share a secret with you, a secret method of teaching the dog to come whenever and

Always end your dog's training sessions with plenty of praise and play time.

wherever he hears you call. I've used this method with thousands of dogs and owners and never found one individual who didn't love to come. It works!

Many dogs owners have told me after only one week of using this method that it's "magic," a "miracle." And this from folks who have, in the past, had no response to the "come" command and dogs that have perpetually attempted to run away or disregard their owners' commands to come.

The secret? Don't teach "come!" Find a new and better way to get the dog interested in getting to your side. As a matter of fact, my little Ginger is ten years old now and has never heard the command "come," yet she races to me like a rocket whenever I call her. I don't have to be in the same room or within her sight when I call. When she hears my voice, she begins running as fast as she can toward the sound of my voice. And she keeps searching until she finds me. Every time she does, she's rewarded with a big celebration from me that often includes a hug and a kiss.

It's called the "Where are you game." I ask the dog a question and through motivation, he quickly learns to answer it. It contains elements of the old hide and seek game, some search behaviors, sound identification exercises, and some speed and stamina components.

Any dog can play the game and any dog, regardless of age or previous response to the "come" command, can learn to love it. I've seen dogs that came when called but crawled to their owners at a snail's pace. But with the "where are you game" those same dogs, after just a few days, began running to their owners. Again, we never teach the word "come."

Unfortunately, it's extremely difficult to put a happy, high-pitched tone to the word "come." Try it for yourself right now. Say out loud, "Come" in as light-hearted a manner as you can. Next, say out loud "Fido? Where are you?" in an equally friendly voice. See what I mean?

The sound of the phrase "Where are you?" ends in an up tone whereas the tone of the word "come" ends in a down sound. This down sound turns off the dog, makes him want to avoid the source of that disagreeable sound.

Before I go any further, let me assure those of you who may contemplate showing your dog in obedience competition at a later day that once you've taught the dog to answer the questions "Where are you?" it's easy to introduce the "Come" command without losing the thrill of the 'Where are you game" he originally learned. And, what's more, he'll come to you like a bat out of — well, you know what I mean!

Now if I've convinced you to at least try the game, let's get started teaching your dog how to play it. We begin with two or three family members plus the dog. (For those who live alone, I'll describe how to play it with only you and your dog in just a moment, so keep reading.)

With the proper training, who knows how far your All-American can go? Little Bentley, a Springer mix owned by Gregory Bryant, flies through the tire jump.

Have several members of the family go into the kitchen. Once there, get out some delicious snacks for the dog such as chunks of cheese, slices of hot dogs, etc. Give each person two or three treats which will be given to the dog later.

While you're preparing the treats, the dog will no doubt know you're working with food and follow you to the kitchen. Don't say anything to the dog, ignore him and talk among yourselves.

While you're there assign each person to a different room in the house. Example: Dad goes to the laundry room, Mom to the hall, and Junior to the dining room. Once the food treats are distributed to each person, leave the kitchen and go to your assigned location.

At this point, you've each got some treats, the dog knows it and will surely follow one of you. Continue to ignore the dog. Just pretend he's not there. Speaking to him now would confuse the dog even more.

As soon as each person is in their assigned spot in the house, call out to one of the people to begin. The beginning person must be one of the people whom the dog *did not* follow.

"Fido? Where are you? Where are you, boy? I've got a goodie. See if you can find me. Where are you?" Be sure that you keep this type of conversation going for as long as it takes the dog to locate the caller. You can say anything you want providing you don't use the word "come" as a command. (I've even used the expression "Come get a cookie. Where are

The time you spend training your mixed breed will result in a close bond between dog and owner.

you?" without a problem simply because the use of the word "come" in that context is exciting and doesn't sound like a command.)

Initially the dog will probably ignore the caller because he doesn't realize that a treat and a celebration are forth coming from the caller. After all, he knows the person he followed has treats and he intends to stick close to the food. However, when the person he's with continues to ignore him (don't look at him or speak to him) he'll get disgusted and eventually decide to check out the caller because that person sounds so exciting. (Little does he realize that the caller has a treat and a celebration waiting for him as well!)

Making this game work depends on the enthusiasm of the callers. When it's their turn to call the dog, they must maintain a constant stream of happy chatter until the dog finds them. It's important to explain to players that the dog will learn to locate them through the sounds of their voices. Asking "Where are you?" once and then just standing there without saying anything won't help the dog find you.

Once the dog locates the first caller, he's rewarded with a treat and lots of happy praise. Remember, he's the winner here and should be treated like a hero with praise and petting.

Now, while all this is going on, the person whom the dog originally followed now moves to a new location, say the living room. Of course the dog will not know

that the first person has changed his location.

As soon as the first person completes his celebration with the dog, the next person begins the same thing, calling excitedly. When the dog realizes that the first celebration is over, he'll perk up his ears and begin to search out the new caller. When he finds caller number two, he'll receive an equally happy celebration of food and praise.

Next, the third person takes his turn at calling the dog. Another celebration follows. By this time, the dog will begin to get the idea that when he hears someone call him and he finds the caller, it's a party. After all, a treat and a short celebration of hugs, petting and play is enough reason for anybody to come!

Now it's time for the original person to call. You remember him. He's the person who began in the laundry room. This is the person whom the dog originally followed and who has now moved to a new location in the living room.

You're about to witness a fascinating event. You're going to see how your dog thinks and reasons. It goes like this: the dog hears the original person calling. He knows that person has food. He remembers being with that person in the laundry room. When he hears the original person calling him excitedly, he races back to the laundry room because that's where the dog left the person. But surprise, the person is gone. Now the dog gets a subtle lesson. Listen to the sounds of the caller's voice and seek out the source of that sound. Don't go back to the original room. Use your ears to follow the sound. Only then will you be successful.

As I said, once the original person begins calling, the dog will race to the laundry room. When he discovers the person is gone, he'll turn and begin following the sound to locate his next celebration.

It's fascinating to watch a dog work out a problem and solve it on his own. And once he does solve it, he is again rewarded. This process serves not only to teach the dog to come when called, it increases his awareness of his environment and his self-esteem. It's like saying, "You're good. You can do anything. You can solve any problem just by using your head!"

This group proves that a "mixed bag" of dogs can exist in one, big, happy family!

By the time all three callers have had a turn, the dog will have figured out how this game works. Then as the callers begin round two, he'll pick up speed as he searches the various rooms of the house for the caller and the next party.

It's important to plan the strategy of the players' movements in advance. Each person should know before the game begins where he intends to hide for each turn. Never hide in the same room for two consecutive turns. Keep moving around the house and challenging the dog's ability to locate you based on his scenting ability to smell you and his hearing ability to recognize your call.

If you play this game regularly and with great enthusiasm, it won't be long before the dog recognizes when you're about to play it and how to find the callers faster and faster. Remember, the faster he finds a caller, the sooner he gets the rewards.

I promised to tell you how to play the game with your dog if you live alone. Here's how it's done: Have a few dog biscuits in your pocket before you begin the game. Then, as you move around the house doing your normal activities, look for opportunities to play when the dog's attention is diverted elsewhere.

Maybe he's playing with a toy, sleeping, or busy looking out a window. Sneak out of the room where the dog is and go to another room in the house. Start calling him with the same questions and happy chatter as described above. Keep calling until the dog finds you.

Amy Rachman teaches her Cockapoo, Coochie, to jump through a hoop.

anyone else. Others don't want their dog to jump on anyone at anytime. If your dog jumps on people, you'll have to decide how you feel about this because most dogs are jumpers, particularly young ones. After all, they only want to get closer to greet you.

There are many ways to teach a dog not to jump on you. Some of those methods are potentially harmful to the dog. Slamming your knee into the dog's chest as he jumps can crack ribs. Stepping on the dog's back feet as he raises his front end into the air can fracture tiny bones in his feet. Both methods aren't particularly successful and usually serve to convince the dog that he doesn't like you because he gets hurt every time he attempts to greet you.

Here's a better way to teach your dog to keep four feet on the ground when greeting you: Allow the dog to jump up on you and when he does, take his front paws in your hands and hold them. Don't squeeze or pinch the paws. Just hold them, and hold them, and hold them some more! In other words, once you take hold of the dog's paws, don't let go.

After a few turns of this, the dog will come racing to find you whenever he hears you ask "Where are you?" If a friend or relative comes to call, recruit them to play the game with you as described earlier for more than one person. It'll be great fun for the dog, and he'll soon become conditioned to finding you in a hurry whenever you call.

As I said earlier, my own Ginger has never heard the command "come" yet she scurries to me whenever I ask the question "Where are you?" She learned as a puppy that getting to me was extremely rewarding and being an opportunist, she never misses a chance for celebration. I stopped giving out treats a long time ago, but it doesn't seem to matter. My praise and attention are reward enough for her.

JUMPING UP

Now, does your dog jump up on people? Some dog owners don't mind the dog jumping on them, but prefer the dog not jump on

Four-month-old Cheezy is a well-behaved Lhasa Apso mix owned by Gayle Kiurski.

Ben, a Border Collie mix owned by Jan Landry, conquers the teeter-totter at an agility trial.

Soon the dog will decide to jump back down, but now he'll discover that his front paws are securely attached to your hands and he can't get down. He'll begin to struggle to get free. As he does, keep holding on.

All the while you're holding his paws, tell him how delighted you are that he came to greet you. Don't reprimand the dog for jumping. Say things like, "What a pretty boy you are. I'm so glad you want to say hello. And look at your pretty brown eyes. Oh, you're such a good boy." Just chatter away in a delighted tone of voice so the dog will realize you're happy to see him and want him to stay up forever. This will soon begin to get tiring to the dog and that's when the jump becomes something less than desirable. Finally, when you think the dog is about to get desperate, let go of his paws and continue to greet him in your happy tone of voice. Chances are the next time the dog rushes to greet you, he'll suddenly recall the hold your hands got on his paws and he'll choose instead to stand wagging his tail and looking up at you. He's learned that jumping on you is dangerous—when you get his front paws in your hands, you never let go.

Be sure to greet him happily when he doesn't jump. If he should attempt another jump, repeat the process until he figures out that keeping his four paws on the ground is much more comfortable and rewarding.

Teaching a dog not to jump on friends and family is easy, too. The next time someone comes to your front door, ask them to wait momentarily until you get your dog under control before you open the door.

With the dog on lead and a biscuit in your hand, go to the door and have the dog sit beside you on your left. Tell him to stay and then reach over to unlock the door, but don't open it. Instead, call out "Come in," to your visitor and hold the dog in a sit position.

Once the caller is inside, hand him or her the biscuit and say, "Now please give this treat to my dog and tell him he's a good boy." Allow the dog to take the biscuit from the visitor and add your own "Good boy."

The dog will busy himself with eating the treat and forget to jump on the visitor. Now escort your guest into your home, say the living room, and continue to have the dog sit beside you as you chat with your guest. Shortly you'll notice the dog calming down. As soon as the dog appears to be under control once again, allow the dog to go to your friend and sniff him in greeting. Let the person pet the dog and talk softly to him so as not to get him too excited again.

When the dog no longer appears to want to crawl all over the guest, remove the lead. At this point, he'll accept the presence of the visitor without wanting to climb all over him.

Within about a week of beginning this controlled greeting program, you'll notice that when the dog hears the doorbell, he'll race to the front door and sit in anticipation of a treat and praise from the visitor. Be prepared, however, to enforce your sit-and-not-jump-for-greeting rule.

There are literally dozens of behaviors we can train the new dog to do, but this would take a whole set of books. The behaviors I've described here are all control exercises that will help you and your dog live peacefully together. None of them is difficult. All of them take time and patience.

TRAINING CLASSES

Your next step should be to enroll in a local obedience class. That's where your dog will learn to listen to you, be well-mannered around other people and dogs, and develop behaviors which will be useful for the rest of his life. But most of all working together in a structured program will help you build a life-long bond together.

Choosing a reputable obedience class is important because there are some that do not use motivational, humane-training methods. In some cases, the instructor just doesn't have enough knowledge and experience to be effective.

The National Association of Dog Obedience Instructors will gladly help you locate a reputable obedience instructor in your area. Write to them for more information and references at PO Box 432, Landing, NJ, 07850-0432.

When searching for a good training facility, be sure the school has a reputation of success using humane methods. Ask your veterinarian, friends, and other dog owners for references. During an eight-week beginners course, dogs should learn to sit, down, stay, come and to walk beside their owners without pulling on the lead. Observe a class in session and evaluate what you see.

Are the dogs happy? Are the owners and dogs working well together? Are the teachers friendly and helpful? As the training hour progresses, does the instructor vary the behaviors they're working on to keep things interesting for dogs and owners? What is the overall atmosphere created by the experience?

Once you've completed a course in basic obedience, you may decide that you and your dog enjoy working together as well as being in the company of others with similar goals. Now is the time to talk to the instructor about continuing the dog's training with the possibility of eventually earning obedience titles for the dog.

If you enroll your dog in a basic obedience class, you will end up with a well-mannered friend that will be welcomed anywhere.

However, if time is at a premium in your life at the moment, you may decide that the basic course was enough and you can't continue. If that's the case, slowly wean the dog off the formal class and daily practice routine.

Warning: Stopping the practice sessions cold turkey style may frustrate your dog when he no longer gets to work with you for that envied praise and attention.

That's when he'll find naughty things to do to get your attention again.

To prevent the dog from obtaining attention caused by unacceptable behavior, practice three times a week for the next three weeks. For two weeks after that, practice twice a week. Then, for the rest of the dog's life, practice once a week.

Scheduling a special time once each week when you and your friend practice obedience behaviors together is good for both of you. Without a periodic review, both of you will eventually forget some of the behaviors and get sloppy at the rest. In addition, the dog will quickly learn to look forward to those treasured special times with you.

Be sure to end every practice session with a period of play and praise. It's also a welcome gesture if you just happen to produce a dog biscuit from your pocket when all the behaviors have been practiced and you're finished for the day. These things tell the dog what a good job he does at being a mannerly and obedient partner.

Most of all, they remind the dog that his leader (you) is still in charge and he'll feel confident knowing that he (the dog) holds an important place in the pack.

SUGGESTED READING

TS-258
TRAINING YOUR DOG FOR SPORTS AND OTHER ACTIVITIES
Charlotte Schwartz
160 pages, over 200 full color photographs

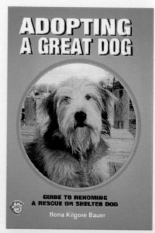

TS-293
ADOPTING A GREAT DOG
Nona Kilgore Bauer
128 pages, over 200 full color photographs

TS-257
CHOOSING A DOG FOR LIFE
Andrew DePrisco & James B. Johnson
Over 800 full color photographs

TS-175
CANINE LEXICON
Andrew DePrisco & James Johnson
896 pages, over 1300 full color photographs

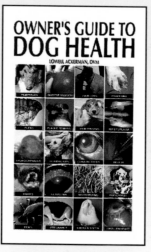

TS-214
OWNER'S GUIDE TO DOG HEALTH
Dr. Lowell Ackerman, DVM
432 pages, over 300 full color photographs

TS-249
SKIN AND COAT CARE FOR YOUR DOG
Dr. Lowell Ackerman, DVM
224 pages, over 190 full color photographs